TOP TIPS:
EXPLAINING THE TRINITY
TO YOUNG PEOPLE

Sarah Bingham and John Grayston

© Scripture Union 2010
First published 2010
ISBN 978 1 84427 396 6

Scripture Union England and Wales
207–209 Queensway, Bletchley,
Milton Keynes, MK2 2 EB, England
Email: info@scriptureunion.org.uk
Website: www.scriptureunion.org.uk

Scripture Union Northern Ireland
157 Albertbridge Road, Belfast, BT5 4PS
Website: www.suni.co.uk

Scripture Union Scotland
70 Milton Street, Glasgow, G4 0HR
Website: www.suscotland.org.uk

Scripture Union Australia
Locked Bag 2, Central Business Coast
Centre, NSW 2252
Website: www.scriptureunion.org.au

Scripture Union USA
PO Box 987, Valley Forge, PA 19482
Website: www.scriptureunion.org

Scripture quotations are taken from
the HOLY BIBLE, NEW INTERNATIONAL
VERSION, (NIV), © 1973, 1978, 1984
by International Bible Society. Used by
permission of Hodder and Stoughton,
a division of Hodder Headline Ltd. All
rights reserved.

The right of Sarah Bingham and John
Grayston to be identified as authors
of this work has been asserted by
them in accordance with the
Copyright and Patents Act 1988.

British Library Cataloguing-in-
Publication Data. A catalogue record
of this book is available from the
British Library.

Printed and bound in Singapore by
Tien Wah Press Ltd

Logo, cover design, internal design:
www.splash-design.co.uk
Internal illustrations: Colin Smithson
Typesetting: Richard Jefferson, Author
and Publisher Services
Advisers: Claire Clinton, Joe Kapolyo,
John Marshall

⤸ Scripture Union is an
international Christian charity working
with churches in more than 130
countries, providing resources to bring
the good news of Jesus Christ to
children, young people and families
and to encourage them to develop
spiritually through the Bible and
prayer.

As well as our network of volunteers,
staff and associates who run holidays,
church-based events and school
Christian groups, we produce a wide
range of publications and support
those who use our resources through
training programmes.

CONTENTS

Introduction   4

Part One   What the Bible says about the Trinity   5

Part Two   The importance of explaining the Trinity   10

Part Three   Explaining the Trinity in practice   18

Ten Top Tips   31

Resources   32

INTRODUCTION

We are dentists, plumbers, teachers, technicians, carpenters, surgeons. We are mothers, sons, aunts, grandfathers. We are gardeners, walkers, photographers, flower arrangers. We define ourselves by our activities and by our relationships.

The Bible defines God in similar ways. We know him through what he does – time and time again his wonderful acts are celebrated. We also experience him in relationship – as our loving Father, as Jesus who shows us the character of God in human form, and as the Spirit who lives out the life of God in those who love him.

We shall attempt to lay out what the Bible says about the way God exists as Father, Son and Spirit and about what that means for our relationship with him. We won't find many easy answers – some may be rather mind-bending. But a sense of mystery and wonder before God is healthy. Who would want to worship a God who could be defined in one neat formula? Would we not rather worship a God who is great and wonderful, profound and mysterious, a God whom we cannot fathom, but a God who meets us in love?

In Part One we'll look at what the Bible says. In Part Two we'll see how Christians have tried to make sense of the Trinity, and in Part Three we will explore how we can explain this to young people. Additional Internet resources are also mentioned. All this is highly relevant to children and adults too!

PART ONE - WHAT THE BIBLE SAYS ABOUT THE TRINITY

One God

The Bible's emphasis is that there is only one God. Deuteronomy 6:1–4 is a basic Jewish statement of faith: The LORD our God, the LORD is one. Jesus identifies this as the great commandment (Mark 12:28–31). The Jewish prophets mock the very idea that the gods of other nations, depicted by wooden or stone idols, even exist (see Isaiah 46:1–7). Paul picks up the same idea when he talks of the Thessalonians turning from idols to serve the living and true God (1 Thessalonians 1:9).

This commitment to worshipping one God (monotheism) was unusual in a world where, in both Old Testament and New Testament times, people worshipped a range of gods. It was hard to be so obviously different and believers were often misunderstood and suffered as a result. Clearly, Jesus and the early Christians believed in and worshipped only one God, the God of Abraham, Isaac and Jacob, who speaks and acts throughout the Old Testament.

This one God revealed himself and was experienced in a range of ways. For example, in the Old Testament, God is described as a Shepherd, Rock, Warrior and Deliverer.

The God and Father of our Lord Jesus Christ

The term 'Father' for God is relatively rare in the Old Testament, but is everywhere in the New Testament. Jesus expresses his own personal relationship with God in these terms, when he uses the language of family intimacy, 'Abba' (Mark 14:36). He refers to the Father over one hundred times in John's Gospel alone, highlighting the closeness of their relationship.

We should not allow the use of the term 'Father' to give the impression that God is male. Father is a metaphor, a picture to help us understand the nature of God and his relationship with humankind. Less frequently, the Bible also uses female metaphors to understand

God. For example, in Isaiah 49:15, God is referred to as a nursing mother.

Initially, only Jesus experiences God as Father but he encourages his followers to share that relationship, but in different ways. His model prayer starts with 'Our Father' (Matthew 6:9). After the resurrection he tells Mary he is going to his Father and her Father (John 20:17). He tells the story of the father who is prepared to let his son have an early share of the inheritance – unthinkable at that time – and receives him back when it's all spent (Luke 15:11–32). We see a picture of God in this forgiving and gracious father.

John writes of the privilege of being the children of God (1 John 1:1–3). We can use the intimate language of childhood, 'Abba' (Romans 8:15–17). We are not children in the same way that Jesus is Son, for he has always been Son, but we are adopted into the family of God (Romans 8:23; Ephesians 1:5).

Paul uses the language of Father sparingly, most frequently in his opening greetings of his letters. He talks of 'the God and Father of our Lord Jesus Christ' (2 Corinthians 1:3; 11:31; Ephesians 1:3). God is 'the Father of all' (Ephesians 4:6).

The Only Begotten Son
Jesus' earliest followers gradually grasped the truth about him. The earliest piece of writing in the New Testament is probably Paul's letter to the Galatians written about AD 48 where he writes that God 'was pleased to reveal his Son in me' (Galatians 1:15,16). Although in the

language of the time, speaking of Jesus as the 'Son of God' did not have to imply he was God, Paul's immediate reference to 'not consulting any human' indicates that he does in some sense mean that Jesus was God.

In Romans 8:3, Paul talks of God sending his Son as a human being, becoming even clearer in Philippians 2:5–11, describing Jesus as 'being in very nature God'. This theme occurs again and again in different ways in Paul's letters, perhaps reaching its clearest expression in Colossians 1:15–20 and 2:9,10.

The writer to the Hebrews writes about God speaking through his Son, who is the 'exact imprint of God's very being' (Hebrews 1:3, NRSV). John also says how 'our fellowship is with the Father and with his Son, Jesus Christ' (1 John 1:3).

The early Christians seem to have had no difficulty in describing Jesus as God's Son, believing this meant that he shared God's very nature, that he was God. They describe him as Lord, using the word from the Greek Old Testament which translates as the personal name of God. For Jews this name was sacred-beyond-utterance. It's hard to grasp how staggering this was: to see Jesus as one with the One God.

This understanding of Jesus could only emerge because it was the claim that Jesus himself made. Many Jewish leaders understood this only too well, which was why they were so set against Jesus (John 5:18). He believed that he had come from the Father in a unique way (John 5:37), claimed that he had been with the Father (John 8:38), and asserted that he and the Father were one (John 10:30). John introduces his Gospel with the astounding claim that the eternal Word who was with God and who was God (John 1:1) had become human and that in him we can see 'the glory as of a father's only son' (John 1:14, NRSV). What's more, during his life Jesus did things that only God could do – gave life, provided food, controlled creation and forgave sins. John concludes his gospel by pointing out that he had written so that readers might also believe that Jesus was the Son of God (John 20:31).

It is always possible to doubt that Jesus was God; but there can be no doubt that that was who he claimed to be. His first followers *and* earliest opponents also believed that was his claim. Thomas, meeting Jesus a week after the Resurrection, immediately declared Jesus to be his Lord and his God (John 20:28). As CS Lewis famously pointed out, Jesus was either mad, bad or God.

Another Counsellor

When Jesus explained to his disciples that he was going back to the Father he promised another Counsellor to come alongside them for ever (John 14:16). He goes on to say 'I will come to you' and 'On that day you will realise that…I am in you'. Jesus is not the Spirit and yet when the Spirit comes, Jesus comes.

Think about…

How do your young people talk about the Spirit? Do they refer to him as God? Do they treat him as a person, someone they can know?

The Spirit is not someone new who suddenly emerges. There are few references to the Spirit in the Old Testament, but there are enough to indicate how he works. The Spirit is there at creation (Genesis 1:2). He is the life-giver, providing what is needed (Psalm 104:27–30). In Psalm 139:7 David recognises that the Spirit is everywhere.

The Spirit provides the creative gifts for the building of the Tent of Meeting (Exodus 31:1–5; 35:30 – 36:1). Moses leads Israel by the Spirit, and when others are appointed to help him, they too receive the Spirit (Numbers 11:16–25). Samson, despite his failures, delivers Israel through the power of the Spirit (Judges 15:14). Kings rule in the power of the Spirit, at least some of the time (1 Samuel 16:13). David is concerned that God will take his Spirit from him (Psalm 51:11).The Spirit comes in power upon prophets and inspires them (Judges 14:6; 1 Samuel 10:10; Ezekiel 11:5). They see a time when the Spirit will do something new (Isaiah 42:1; Ezekiel 37:1–14; Joel 2:28–32).

Joel's prophecy is fulfilled at Pentecost (Acts 2:1–21). But before that, John the Baptist points to the coming of Jesus who will 'baptise you with the Holy Spirit' (Mark 1:8). Jesus promises the coming of the Spirit to empower the church for its mission (Acts 1:1–8). He commands his disciples to make disciples, baptising them in the name of the Father, the Son and the Holy Spirit (Matthew 28:19); the mission is that of God but equally that of Father, Son and Spirit.

Throughout Acts, the Spirit gives the energy to the mission of the church, God's mission. The early Christians are encouraged to believe that they have new life through the Spirit. Romans 8:1–17 is an important passage where God, Jesus and the Spirit are all seen to be intimately involved in giving us life, and enabling us to live as new people. Their roles are not identical; yet what God does, Jesus does and the Spirit does.

This pattern is repeated again and again. For example, see 2 Corinthians 13:14, where Paul urges the church in Corinth to enjoy 'the grace of the Lord Jesus Christ, and the love of God, and the fellowship of the Holy Spirit', a verse many churches use as a concluding prayer.

2

PART TWO - THE IMPORTANCE OF EXPLAINING THE TRINITY

Making sense of it all

During the first four centuries of the Christian church there were many attempts to produce a definition that neatly summarised the Trinity. This started with the ideas of threeness and oneness. How could they be reconciled? In some circles, especially in the eastern churches (around the Balkans, Eastern Europe, Asia Minor, the Middle East, Northeastern Africa and southern India), they tended to emphasise the three, so much so that at times it looked as though Christians believed in three gods.

In others circles, especially in the churches of Western Europe, the one God was emphasised to the point where the Son and the Spirit were just ways in which the One revealed himself at different points in human history. In its extreme form this was condemned as the heresy called modalism. The complex discussion is tied up with the nature of Jesus' divinity, further complicated by differences in language, including discussions about how the three related to one another.

In the western church, the tendency was to speak of one substance and three persons. In some ways this serves as a helpful definition. But it has become less helpful today where the word 'person' has taken on a different meaning. When we speak of a person we are thinking of an independent-acting individual. This was not what was intended by those who coined the language in the second century.

An uneasy agreement between the different understandings was

> **In reality...**
> A Jehovah's Witness who had knocked at the door of one of the authors was surprised by the response to the description of God as 'one substance, three persons'. "So God's like a schizophrenic with three personalities, then?"

reached at the Council of Nicea in AD 325. Further discussions were held at the Council of Constantinople in AD 381. While some focused on the origins of the Son and the Spirit, Augustine of Hippo (AD 354–430) argued that the three were differentiated not by their origins but by their relationships. God was One who had existed in the relationship of Father, Son and Spirit, from all eternity.

As a result of this debate, the church came to understand the Bible to be saying that the One God has always existed as Father, Son and Spirit, bound together in a relationship of mutual love and indwelling one another (John 17:5). They cannot be divided. The Father, Son and Spirit have a common will and purpose. The Spirit does not go off and do things on his own. When God acts, Father, Son and Spirit act. And yet they act in different ways. The Father does not go to the cross – but is totally involved. It is the Spirit who works in the lives of individual believers, but the Father and Son are actively involved.

> **Think about...**
> Using an Internet search engine, find the Athanasian Creed, written in the fifth century AD. The language may be hard but reflect on this creed.

Long-standing misunderstandings

Here are some misconceptions that people you meet may express:

- Division: this person talks and thinks as though the three had separate wills and minds (like the Jehovah's Witness, see page 10)
- Tritheism: this person takes an extreme form of dividing the three persons of the Trinity
- Merging: this person denies the threeness, in theory or in practice
- Modalism: this person holds the idea that God appears at different times in different forms – appearing as Father in the Old Testament, as Jesus in the Gospels and as the Spirit in the age of the church

- Confusion: this person ignores the difference of function, which in practice shows itself in prayers like, 'Thank you, Father, for dying for us…' See page 19 for an explanation.

The implications of a Trinitarian God

It's a mystery
We cannot penetrate the mystery of the Trinity. But remember, God has chosen to reveal himself in three persons. He is not deliberately obscuring himself from us.

There is no way we can understand God and, quite frankly, if we could understand God, would he be worth worshipping? Our attempts at explanation can all too often make God look like a magnified human being. The revelation of God as both one and three reminds us that there are things that we do not understand. So, in the explanations below, don't expect everything to be crystal clear but hopefully some things will be clearer.

One of the great problems of humanity is that we often think that we know everything and can do everything. A good dose of humility helps us keep things in perspective. God is great, awesome and all-powerful. We are not. As King Solomon prayed, 'The heavens, even the highest heavens, cannot contain you' (2 Chronicles 6:18). The idea of the mystery of God calls for humility.

The Trinity calls us to worship
Christian worship is centred on God – Father, Son and Spirit – originating in the love of the Father, made possible through the relationship we have through the Son and inspired by the Spirit. This is most obvious in our language of prayer. Children and young people are often natural worshippers so for their part can help adults focus

expectantly upon God in all his fullness. Youth leaders, however, can intentionally encourage young people to pray openly to the Trinity; to be empowered by the Spirit, aware of the love they receive from the Father and looking for evidence of what Jesus has done.

Think about...
Who do you worship in personal prayer or when you stand or kneel with young people worshipping God. What images do you hold in your mind and are they helpful?

The Trinity invites us to join the family

Father, Son and Spirit have always existed in perfect relationship. As humans created in the image of God we share that desire for relationship and the ability to relate to others and indeed to God. Sadly when human beings rebelled against God they broke their relationship with him, one that was their birthright (or creation-right). Amazingly, God wants to restore that relationship. We are invited to share in the life of the Trinity, to become sons and daughters by adoption. This is something to hold on to in a world in which many people, including children and young people, lack any sense of belonging. It can give a new understanding of human identity, to know who we are 'in God'. Of course, this will affect the ability to relate to other people too.

In reality...
A woman who as a child had been abused by her father worked hard at the model of Fatherhood revealed in Scripture to grasp how God sees her. This enabled her to pray for her earthly father, wanting to see her family restored to what it should have been.

The Trinity acts in salvation

Jesus does save. But so do the Father and the Spirit. The Father, in love, sends the Son, who, in love, comes to live as a man, conceived through the Spirit (Matthew 1:18), inspired and empowered by the Spirit (Matthew 12:18,28; Luke 4:14), finally giving himself, in love, through the Spirit (Hebrews 9:14). The Son is raised by the power of the Spirit 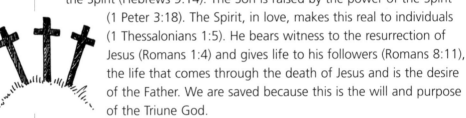 (1 Peter 3:18). The Spirit, in love, makes this real to individuals (1 Thessalonians 1:5). He bears witness to the resurrection of Jesus (Romans 1:4) and gives life to his followers (Romans 8:11), the life that comes through the death of Jesus and is the desire of the Father. We are saved because this is the will and purpose of the Triune God.

The Trinity changes people

Concern about God's plan for their lives can be a problem for young people, thinking about further education, jobs and life partners. We all need reminding of God's plan for our lives, 'to shape the lives of those who love him along the same lines as the life of his Son' (Romans 8:29, *The Message*). God intends us to be like Jesus. The Father desires it, the Son is the ultimate role model and the Spirit makes it happen. The Spirit is often referred to as the Holy Spirit, partly because he demonstrates that holiness is the character of God and partly because he enables us to share in that holiness. He is the One who produces the fruit of changed character in our lives (Galatians 5:22,23).

Many young people find it hard being different from their peers. It is hard to stand out and even harder to actually behave in a distinctly different way. It can be liberating to understand that this is the will of God, achieved through co-operating with the activity of the Spirit.

The Trinity calls for care of creation

Many people care deeply about the environment, for reasons of self interest, an affinity with animals or plants, making sure the planet will be habitable for future generations or a mystical idea that we are all part of the one.

As Christians we care for the environment primarily because God made it, the Son sustains it and cares for it and it is one realm in which the Spirit works. God said, "Let us make humankind in our image" (Genesis 1:26, NRSV). Children have a natural sense of wonder at creation. Young people are often passionate about issues related to the environment. We can help them to understand where God is at work in his creation.

The Trinity sends us on a mission

Jesus instructed his first disciples to make more disciples, and to baptise them in the name of the Father, the Son and the Holy Spirit (Matthew 28:19). Notice incidentally that it is the singular 'name', where we might expect 'names', plural – an interesting indication of three being one.

Think about...

How are you helping those in your youth group to express the reality of the Trinity among their friends and local community?

Mission is God's idea and it is thoroughly Trinitarian. The Father's mission to the world involves the sending of the Son and then sending the Church to act in the power of the Spirit. It is the Spirit who directs our mission and who provides the necessary power. It is the Spirit who convicts people of their need and brings them to faith in Jesus (John 16:8).

When we long for children and young people to come to faith we are simply reflecting the love of God, Father, Son and Spirit and carrying out his purpose in the world. It is never our business to convert people – that is the work of the Spirit (John 3:6). It means we do not put pressure on anyone to come to Jesus, least of all children. We simply observe what the Spirit is doing.

We shall often find that the Spirit has been at work long before we get there. It is not that he works with us, but that we work with him as he carries out the purposes of God. So whenever we engage with the community or with the wider world, the first question to ask is, 'What is the Spirit doing already? Where are there indications of love, of

In reality...

A Christian woman befriended the new family who moved in next door. Without realising it, she began to answer the deep questions that the 14-year-old girl in this family was asking. The girl sensed God speaking to her through this woman. She eventually put her trust in him. Before she moved home, the Holy Spirit was already active in her life.

justice, of sacrifice? How might these become bridges for the good news about Jesus?'

The Trinity affects dialogue with other faiths

Mission in a modern multi-faith world presents special problems, since people of other faiths have different perspectives on God. For example, our understanding that God is three-in-one differentiates Christians from the other great monotheistic world faiths, Judaism and Islam. Both believe that there is only one God and that he exists as unity rather than trinity. The Christian view is especially problematic for Muslims. Muhammad lived in an environment where the Christian position had become very close to three separate gods, which is one reason why he and his followers have placed such a prominent emphasis on one God. When talking to Jews and Muslims we need to clearly explain that we too believe in one God and that he is truly one, but also be prepared to explain that we believe that the one God comes to us as Father, Son and Spirit.

Hindus, at a practical level, believe in the existence of many gods and the idea of Father, Son and Spirit is no problem. On the other hand, they believe that there is one ultimate reality that can be experienced yet has come in many different forms. This understanding of ultimate reality tends to be impersonal so we need to explain that we believe in one God, who is personal and who delights in relationship.

> **In reality…**
> During lessons in one Jewish school on 'what is a Christian?' every class had at least one question about how the Trinity could really be 'One God'.

> **Think about…**
> Who will have a more sophisticated view of God; a 14-year-old unchurched young person or a 9-year-old Muslim child? How will someone's pre-conceived ideas about God affect their ability to understand or accept the idea of Trinity?

In conclusion
The Trinity is a mystery, but also a truth that affects the whole of our faith – our salvation, our worship, our lifestyle, our mission. Understood correctly the Trinity will lead us to praise and worship, and to obedience. The challenge is how to help children and young people better understand God. Read on…

3

PART THREE – EXPLAINING THE TRINITY IN PRACTICE

Who we are talking with

How we explain the Trinity will depend on such factors as the age and background of the person or group and the context of the discussion. An 8-year-old has a much weaker grasp of non-literal language or abstract ideas than an 18-year-old. Someone with English as a second language may fail to grasp precise meaning. A Hindu child will have a different concept of what is meant by the phrase 'Son of God' or 'God the Son' to a child from a Christian, secular or Muslim background. A question about the Trinity at the end of an act of collective worship may be answered differently when asked at a Christian after-school club or in an RE lesson.

> **In reality...**
> A children's worker said, 'I remember a 5-year-old who, on being told that God the Father sent his Son, Jesus to the world, said "Then there could be one up there and one down here, couldn't there!"'

The language we use

Prayer and discussion
God just wouldn't be God if human beings could understand him. However, he has partially revealed himself in a variety of ways that we can understand, in order that people can build a relationship with him. This may explain why God presents himself differently to people throughout the Old Testament – in a burning bush, a pillar of fire and a hand writing on a wall, for example. Titles like creator, saviour, judge and husband offer understandable concepts to give some insight into what God is like. The Trinity basically causes us problems because we literally cannot comprehend how three persons can be one Person.

Two things can help people enter the mystery. First, we can ensure our worship and prayer is Trinitarian. Include hymns and songs that speak of the Trinity. For example, the chorus of 'There is a redeemer'. Use prayer language that addresses God as Father, Son and Spirit. There are some rich resources to use from the past.

You may have found yourself praying like this: 'Father, thank you for coming to Earth in the form of Jesus. Thank you for dying to save us.' This is muddled thinking. We pray to all the members of the Trinity and although God isn't 'picky', it shows we are thinking who God is if, when we pray, we ascribe the right actions and attributes to the right person. So, thank Jesus for coming, living, dying and rising. Thank the Spirit for comfort, guidance and being with us. Thank the Father for creation, sending Jesus and building the church. Remember that in Romans 8:26 we read that the Spirit intercedes on our behalf when we cannot find words to talk with God (and presumably to even address him!).

Secondly, when talking about God, make regular use of terms such as, 'God, the Father, the Son and the Holy Spirit'. It may not make sense to everyone, but understanding the Trinity is never easy.

> **Think about...**
> Is the language about the Trinity that you use with your youth group too simplistic or too complex, too abstract or too literal?

Models, metaphors and similes

We try to explain the Trinity using terms, at least mentally, like 'model', 'metaphor' and 'simile'. But all of these have their limitations. See pages 21–30 for some examples and explanation.

- A model – if we build a model from a kit, we expect it to be an accurate, but small-scale, representation of the 'real thing'. Models of the Trinity do not work that way! Maybe we should drop the word 'model'.

- A metaphor – this uses picture language to explain or illuminate meaning which can lead to confusion. For example, the phrase 'Be the fire in my heart' in the song 'Jesus be the centre' might literally imply flames inside the body. We are not speaking literally of Jesus frying internal organs!

- A simile – many ways to explain the Trinity involve similes to suggest 'the Trinity is like… (something else)'. We must explain that any simile is only partially accurate. Each will have elements that do not accurately reflect the nature of God. So, when we try to explain the Trinity, we use the best examples we can, but explain that they are not fully accurate.

Potentially every explanation is heretical if we leave people thinking this is the 'whole picture' of what God is like. In your teaching present things carefully, using a phrase such as 'In some ways, God is a bit like…'. We may need to help young people see one thing in the picture that does *not* describe God well. For example, ice, water and steam are like God because the same material is in three separate forms doing three things all at the same time. But it is *not* like God because ice, water and steam cannot love and interact with each other.

In reality…

A vicar was in the local church school just before Trinity Sunday. To explain the Trinity, he had three PE hoops taped together in an overlapping pattern. Everyone ended up confused. Don't try to simplify things that cannot be explained!

It may be that the best term we can use is to say, 'One picture of the Trinity is…' A picture only ever represents reality. It is not the full reality. Pictures are also open to interpretation and carry layers of meaning.

Using a variety of pictures about the Trinity

It is important to be comfortable with and use more than one picture of the Trinity. The pictures you use should reflect all that you know about the person who is asking or who you are talking with. A number of pictures are suggested here, including some that lend themselves to an active exploration of the concept of Trinity with a group. Some will be for thinking about, some for looking at and some for creative exploration! The limitations of each picture below are also noted.

Pictures from cooking and food

Cooking often involves mixing and then baking ingredients to create something different.

- A fruit cake or pastry, but, if for obvious reasons, emphasising the 'threeness' of God, only three ingredients are used (using a standard recipe), the cake will be very bland. Pancake batter is better since it is made from egg, flour and milk and is easier to make. But even here it is bland without salt and fillings.
- Trifle – often made of jelly, custard and cream (though some people like sponge and fruit as well).
  Note: any picture where three materials are still visible (like the trifle), rather than mixed together (like the pancake), may be interpreted by those with a Muslim background as meaning the Trinity as three separate gods.
- Mars bars – made of chocolate, caramel and nougat – each ingredient is delicious, but the combination is better than the three individual components.

- An egg – comprises of shell, white and yolk – each part can be described as 'egg', though an egg is incomplete without all three parts. This picture can be extended by explaining that God came in visible human form (like the shell) but was broken in order that, amongst other things, the spirit could be released over everyone. *Note:* both white and yolk are released when the shell is broken! Another weakness is that when cooking, one part is always discarded and sometimes the white and yolk are separated.

Pictures from the natural world
- The three physical states of water – ice, water and steam – three apparently different materials, but of the same 'stuff' or 'substance'. *Note:* in temperate climates like the UK, it is almost impossible to get all three states at once. However, they do co-exist around geysers in Iceland or Yellowstone Park or in cold climates, where the sun shining on melting ice can lead to steam evaporating. With Internet access, show a clip of all three to illustrate the point.
- A rose – comprises of the physical flower, the colour and the scent.
- The sun – a ball of gas which we experience as warmth and light.
- An elephant – described as like a tree trunk (legs), a rope (tail) and palm leaf (ear), but is one creature of many parts.
  Note: it is only one personality, not three. This image is based on a poem by John Saxe, where six blind men feel an elephant and each describes it differently. It could be said this makes the Trinity a hexity!
- White light – splits into every rainbow colour.
  Note: mixing just *three* colours of light – red, blue and green – makes white light.

- The three-lobed leaf of a shamrock (clover also works) – shows how three could be one. St. Patrick is said to have used this.
- Three drops of water on a plate – each drop is the same substance, and size. By tilting the plate, the three drops come together to make one drop. Three in one!
  Note: the three individual drops are no longer identifiable. This may give a blurred perception.
- A chord of three notes – provides a tangible example of three elements, each able to be experienced in isolation, combining to make a separate entity whilst remaining individual elements. If the note of C is played, the note fills the air; the combined sound of C and E fills the air; but a richer, fuller sound is experienced if a third note (G or the higher C) is added. Each note is the same substance (vibrating air molecules), yet has a separate identity. In combination, the three are synergistic (more than the three isolated elements). A variation of this is one note played along with the same note one octave above and one below – three notes that are the same, yet distinct.

In reality...
Brass players commonly play two notes together by accident, 'splitting' a note. One horn player, who was also a trained singer, could play a chord on her horn by deliberately splitting a note in a controlled way and singing a third note into the horn – an unusual and ear-catching sound!

Pictures from man-made objects
These are objects where three different materials or parts can still be seen when the 'whole' is made:

- A Russian wedding ring – made of three strands of gold – white, yellow and red – bonded together.
- A tricolour flag – such as the French or Italian ones, where one flag is made of three different coloured fabrics.
- The word 'one' – comprises three letters – o,n,e – but is a single word. Individually, each letter carries little or no meaning, but when combined, they make perfect sense.

Here are pictures from objects that have three parts that are integral to the whole object:

- A three-legged stool – only stable when the legs are of equal length and strength.
- An electrical plug (in the UK) – only works if all three pins are plugged into the socket.
  Note: sometimes the earth wire is not connected but power flows nonetheless.
- In a trick, a magician apparently turns three ropes into one rope. (This is a good visual example if you can find someone who can do the trick but remember to explain that God is not an illusionist out to trick us.)
- One candle flame – fills the space in a dark room, though the light will be quite dim. A second and third flame brought together with the first does not mean more space is filled, but raises the light intensity. Whilst the flames are the same, the separateness is retained, which may confuse the association of three-in-oneness. A better picture may be given by using one candle with three wicks.

Explore three-in-oneness using two common methods:

- Plaiting together three strands to make a bangle or friendship bracelet. Alternatively, try plaiting and baking bread or cookie dough, then eating it together in a communion service. This reminds those involved of the different parts of the Trinity – the Father sent the Son to die as the sacrifice and the Holy Spirit filled all who live Jesus' resurrection life.

- A group stands in a circle throwing three balls of coloured wool to each other to make a unique weaving. Once complete, it is hard to extricate one strand without destroying the whole.

Real paintings and sculptures

Medieval and pre-medieval artists designed visual representations of the Trinity:

- A common image from Europe and Asia is of three hares (drawn or carved) dancing in a circle. Each hare appears to have two ears, but there are only three ears in total. Each is integral to the image of the other two. (See www.chrischapmanphotography.com/hares for photos of this design.) Connecting this design with the Trinity came a long time after the image was first conceived.
- A Medieval Swiss picture, where a figure is portrayed with three overlapping faces. (See http://photo.net/photodb/photo–photo_id=7668907.)
- Molecule Man 1+1+1 by Jonathan Borofsky in the Yorkshire Sculpture Park or in Berlin, where three figures are joined together but only two can be clearly seen at one time, with parts of one body shared by another. (See www.sculpture.org/documents/parksdir/p&g/yorkshir/york1.shtml.) Further artistic representations are in Resources on page 32.

Pictures from shapes or maths

You do not need to be a mathematician to relate to these pictures and many young people will relate to them!
Note: all these pictures lack personality and relationships.

- How can the three persons in the Trinity equal one – 1+1+1 = 1? (This question ignores the fact that God is not bound by the laws of physics or maths.) In base ten maths that we use daily, 1+1+1 is not 1. However, if we calculate 1x1x1, the answer is 1.
  Note: This picture is impersonal and might be seen to imply God is multiplying. It may be a legitimate answer to the initial question, which is commonly asked by Jehovah's Witnesses.

  In reality...
  A Maths teacher says, 'My GCSE students get 1x1x1 = 1. Three one's are separate units but combined together they don't make three but rather one!'

- Here are three lines / \ __. They are separate and useful, but when brought together make a whole. Each retains its individuality, which is only complete when all three are linked to form a triangle. △

- Every solid object in the physical universe exists in three spatial dimensions – length, depth and breadth. Looking at an object from three vantage points will produce three very different descriptions of the same object.

- The tricele symbol to represent eternity used by the Ancient Celts, later became identified with the Trinity. This comprises of a continuous line woven into a simple three-looped knot, with a circle woven through it.

- The mathematical construction called the *Borromean Rings* – important because they demonstrate properties hard to explore through other means. The importance of this construction as a picture of the Trinity is that each ring is so interlocked with the other two, that removal of one destroys the whole thing. Thus, there are three clearly distinctive parts, but no 'whole' remains if one piece is removed.

Pictures from people or personality

- An individual human being can be defined through their relationship to others – the nature of the Trinity is completely dependent on relationship. One person can be a son, dad and brother or a mother, aunt and cousin.
  Note: the 'threeness' is defined by external relationships, rather than inherent to the person being described.

- Many children of immigrants in the UK have three names – one in English, one in their 'heart language', and a nickname for family use only. They have three names, but are 'one'.
  Note: God is one, but also three, not just one referred to by using three different names.

- Identifying different elements that make us 'whole' beings – most commonly used elements today are probably 'mind, body and spirit'. Many bookshops have a MBS section and there are many MBS fairs. This picture identifies people as having mental faculties, physical bodies and a spiritual nature. A similar, but less commonly used picture is of body, spirit and soul.

- Our conscious self – intellect, emotions and actions – connects mind, spirit (or soul) and body as an integrated being.

- To be a 'whole' person, a personality must be able to communicate. But a robot that communicates (eg auto-generated email answer) is not a person as it does not have personality.
  Note: as programming gets better, some computers/robots have

the appearance of personality, which would blur the definition of 'person'. Some people with profound and multiple disabilities, or with severe autism or those who have suffered major injury or illness may still display personality without being able to communicate. We are unlikely to say they are not a 'person' despite failing the 'test' implicit in this picture.

A fundamental issue with all these pictures (as with ice, water and steam) is that it would be easy to slip into modalism (seeing God as presenting a different face in different contexts) and define the persons of the Trinity by paralleling their expression with the different dimensions of personhood exhibited by people. (For example, Father = mind, Son = body, Spirit = spirit.) Many of these pictures based on people address the fundamental limitation of all the other pictures, because they feature personality and relationship. However, they are still limited in the understanding they convey, especially in that the relationships are between separate people, not persons within one Person.

Pictures based on relationships

* 'The shield of the Trinity' – a physical representation of the relationships within the Trinity based on a medieval diagram which is shaped by the Athanasian creed – see page 11.
  Note: this may work well for those who learn visually, but may also seem to imply the Father as being of greater importance than the Son or the Spirit.

- The team pursuit race in cycling (for men) has a team of four chasing another team of four over a long distance. The race is won by the team whose third member crosses the line first. Members of the team take it in turn to lead, as this takes most energy and effort. In the closing stages, one member often takes the lead and rides at an all-out sacrificial speed to boost the team, then drops out. Their effort allows the third team member to cross the line in a quicker time. So there's one team, with three riders to cross the line, all making an effort and playing their part.
  Note: four people are involved.
- A musical trio comprises three musicians – each plays their own line of music, but the composition depends on all three lines being played at once, equally complementing and enhancing each other. This is similar to the relationships between the sections of an orchestra.
- An allegorical story – three people can stand outside a house and honestly say, 'That's my house.' One would be the architect who designed it, one is the builder who built it and one is the owner who lives in it. Sometimes three roles can be found in one person. God designed us, formed us and lives within us.
- Two people who marry become 'one' – a biblical model. This is not just one flesh, but a depth of relationship where 'though they remain as two individuals, they are so united in heart, mind, body and

Think about…

Some people have been upset by the startling portrayal of the Trinity in *The Shack* by William Paul Young (Hodders). Others are touched by the way their relationship is revealed. This might be a good discussion starter.

spirit that we say they have become one' (Mark Williamson from *History Makers*).

Note: The Trinity, even closer in relationship, involves three, not two.

- Dancing around – the early church fathers developed the image of relationships within the Trinity for what they termed 'perichoreisis' (literally 'dancing around'). It carries connotations of being in the same place at the same time doing the same thing in a way that weaves the participants literally in and out of each other. Looking at a circle dance from above, the unity of movement and purpose is striking. Only on closer inspection would individual dancers become visible. In country dancing there is a particular type of spin where a gentleman and his two lady partners weave around each other in a pattern. This may be one of our best pictures of how the Trinity inter-relates.

- Rublev's icon – three figures with identical faces sit around a table revealing relationships, interest, attention, service, equality and unity, among other things. There is significance in colours, postures, background and what each holds. This can be found at www.wellsprings.org.uk/rublevs_icon/rublev.htm.

You may feel overwhelmed by all these pictures of the Trinity. However, you should have found some that work for you and will connect with the young people you are in contact with. No picture is perfect, but maybe this mosaic of imagery helps to grasp something more about God, and gives us a glimpse of how little we actually understand.

TEN TOP TIPS

- Remember, none of us can fully understand God. He is a mystery.

- Work hard at expanding and enriching your own understanding of the Trinity - see the Resources section, page 32.

- Make sure that your worship and prayer activities include the Trinity and intentionally use different names to address God.

- When you talk about God, at least sometimes, talk about him as Father, Son and Spirit.

- Be aware that children and young people are influenced by their backgrounds so any child from another faith background will not see God as Trinity. Many young people have little awareness of God.

- Try to use Biblical stories as often as you can.

- Remember to explain the limitations of the pictures you use and try not to over-complicate things.

- Remember children find mystery easier to accept than adults do.

- Listen to what the children or young people share of their experience and share your own experiences of God.

- Be flexible and be humble!

RESOURCES

Websites with visual examples

Rublev icon: www.wellsprings.org.uk/rublevs_icon/rublev.htm
The Pedroso Murillo: www.nationalgallery.org.uk/cgi-bin/
El Greco's 'Holy Trinity': www.abcgallery.com/E/elgreco/elgreco18.html
Three Hare imagery: www.chrischapmanphotography.com/hares/
Geysers showing ice, water and steam: www.geysergazing.com/
Tricele: www.faithclipart.com/image/gold-trimmed-celtic-trinity-knot.html
Molecule Man 1+1+1 by Jonathan Borofsky in the Yorkshire Sculpture Park: www.sculpture.org/documents/parksdir/p&g/yorkshir/york1.shtml

Further reading

More accessible

Tim Chester, *Delighting in the Trinity*, Monarch, 2005
Steve Hutchinson, *So, why God?*, Scripture Union, 2007 (12 sessions for a midweek children's club to explore who God is)
Alister McGrath, *Understanding the Trinity*, Kingsway, 1987
Stuart Olyott, *The Three are One*, Evangelical Press, 1979
Robert Willoughby, *So, who is God?* Scripture Union, 2006 (for 8–11s, 30 questions children ask about God)

More challenging

Brian Edgar, *The Message of the Trinity*, IVP, 2004
Colin Gunton, *Father, Son and Holy Spirit*, T & T Clark Publishers, 2003
Robert Letham, *The Holy Trinity*, P & R Publishing, 2004
Ben Witherington III and Laura M. Ice, *The Shadow of the Almighty*, Wm. B. Eerdmans Publishing Company, 2002